INCREDIBLE FEATS

Raising the stakes. These people really know how to push the boundaries. Read about the man who locked himself inside a washing machine, the girl who had 25 snails on her face, and the skydivers who formed a diamond shape in the sky the size of a football field.

Rob Thomson from New Zealand traveled 7,500 mi (12,000 km) around the world on a skateboard.

WATERFALL *Riders*

Paddling a kayak down a tranquil river may be fun for some, but real thrill-seekers look for something a little more demanding. Those who can overcome their fear, after looking down at the white water below, brave the rocks and ride down crashing waterfalls.

Extreme kayaker Pat Keller of North Carolina plunged down the boiling waters of the 120-ft (36.5-m) La Paz waterfall in Costa Rica, looking like flotsam and jetsam in the deluge. He plummeted over the edge of the waterfall at the equivalent of around 300 ft (91 m) a minute. Once over the falls, Pat would have been dragged under the water before resurfacing.

Kayakers use different techniques, and at La Paz Pat rode the waterfall in the center of its 10-ft (3-m) width, so that he had the maximum amount of water on each side. Pat used a curved round-bow boat that measured about 8 ft (2.5 m long), and was made of polyethylene plastic. It was buoyant and helped him resurface quickly.

Pat paddled away from his amazing endeavor, but broke his hand badly in the fierce impact at the bottom of the thundering falls. Later, he had to have surgery to correct the damage.

Pat appears exhilarated, despite his broken hand, after kayaking down La Paz waterfall.

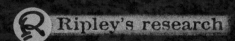

Ripley's research

HOW IS IT DONE?

Kayaks used in extreme kayaking are often made from toughened yet flexible fiberglass to prevent shattering. They are being made shorter than they used to be and this increases the rider's control in the turbulent water, helps avoid them getting stuck in dangerous rock crevices and adds strength on impact after a steep drop.

Each stretch of water attempted is scouted out beforehand and the best line of attack planned to give the kayaker the best chance of making it out the other side. Special techniques are required using the paddle to steer out of danger: a "boof" is pulling a wheelie in a kayak, lifting the nose in a sharp shift of direction, either bouncing off a rock or in water. A high level of physical strength and fitness is also needed to maneuver the short boats to keep the nose up and prevent the craft submerging.

When extreme kayakers face a steep drop, they position their body over the kayak and hold their paddle close in, to prevent their spine taking the impact and avoid shoulder dislocations caused by the paddle pulling away from the body. Tucking close to the kayak with an arm over the face—known as the crash position—prevents the equipment from smacking into the kayaker's head as the water hits. A technique often used on the big drops is to "pencil" into the water in a vertical position to limit impact.

Another of the world's top extreme kayakers, fearless Jesse Combs of Oregon, risked life and limb by paddling down the Mesa Falls in Idaho, facing violent currents and sharp rocks 70 ft (21 m) below.

KAYAKING CAPERS

❯ Shaun Baker has paddled over a waterfall with a 65-ft (19.8-m) vertical drop, traveled at 40 mph (63 km/h) on snow, and sped down huge sand dunes in the Sahara Desert, all in a kayak.

❯ Solo kayaker Satoru Yahata from Okinawa, Japan, arrived in Taiwan on June 18, 2007, after setting off from the Philippines, 435 mi (700 km) away, 16 days earlier. Yahata, in an 18-ft (5.5-m) kayak, was the first solo kayaker to successfully complete the trip.

❯ Extreme kayaker Tyler Bradt paddled down a 107-ft (33-m) descent over Alexandra Falls, Canada, and didn't flip once.

❯ Two British men were rescued from the North Sea when their attempt to cross the stretch of water from Scotland to the Faroe Islands in a kayak was cut short by bad weather and ill health. They hoped to row nonstop for 50 to 70 hours to complete the 220-mi (355-km) voyage.

❯ In 2001, British adventurer Pete Bray paddled a kayak across the Atlantic Ocean, braving frequent storms, gales, and broken equipment, to complete the 2,892-mi (4,800-km) trip.

Nine-year-old Tiana Walton from Cheshire, England, managed to fit 25 garden snails on to her face at once. The slimy creatures covered her eyes, nose, and mouth. "It was relaxing," she said, "but it felt a bit cold. They were quite smelly and you could see their big, long eyes."

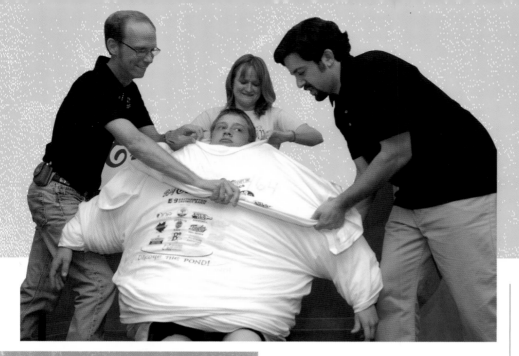

Tight Fit

Austin D. Crow, age 12, of Easthampton, Massachusetts, wore no fewer than 168 T-shirts at the same time—and became so wide that he couldn't make it through the door of his house. It took him nearly three hours to get dressed and the shirts—the largest of which were size 7X—weighed more than 80 lb (36 kg). Austin himself weighed only 111 lb (50 kg).

POWER OF PRAYER ■ Reverend Les Davis of Headland, Alabama, possesses such strong jaws that he can bend steel bars in his teeth.

BIG PICNIC ■ In 2008, a woolen mill in Pembrokeshire, Wales, took three weeks to create a picnic blanket that weighed one ton and was large enough to cover four tennis courts.

FLYING VISIT ■ A U.S. pilot keeps her long-distance relationship alive by making 8,318-mi (13,386-km) round trips to visit her husband in Scotland twice a month. Donna Clark uses planes, trains, buses, cars, and ferries to make the 24-hour, 4,159-mi (6,693-km) trip from Cleveland, Ohio, to the remote Isle of Skye, where husband Bryan is a hotel manager.

TREE PLANTING ■ Around 300 villagers in Assam, India, planted 284,000 saplings in 24 hours in July 2008.

BUSINESS CARDS ■ Ryan John DeVries of Sarnia, Ontario, Canada, has been collecting business cards for longer than 20 years and has accumulated more than 224,000.

BASEBALL SHRINE ■ Paul Jones of Las Vegas, Nevada, started collecting baseball cards in 1997 and now has a collection of more than 520,500. He also collects photos of players and autographed baseballs.

ELVIS TOUR ■ Elvis Presley fan Matt Hale from Hertfordshire, England, spent a year traveling the world dressed as his hero—in a white jumpsuit, black bouffant wig, and shades. He joined in Brazil's Rio Carnival, posed next to the statues on Easter Island, and trekked to the lost Inca city of Machu Picchu in Peru.

FILM FAN ■ Retired painter and decorator Gwilym Hughes, from Dolgellau, Wales, has watched over 28,000 movies in his lifetime. The first movie he ever saw was *King Solomon's Mines*, starring Deborah Kerr and Stewart Granger, and he also has more than 1,000 books on the subject of cinema.

BASEBALL ODYSSEY ■ Josh Robbins of Redondo Beach, California, visited all 30 Major League baseball parks in just 26 days in 2008. Starting in Seattle, Washington, on June 16 and finishing in Milwaukee, Wisconsin, on July 11, he traveled 14,212 mi (22,870 km) and spent more than $2,000 on gas.

DEADLY COMPANIONS ■ At a zoo in Hartbeespoort Dam, South Africa, Martin Smit spent 113 days in a glass enclosure with 40 deadly snakes.

JUNK RACER ■ Two Chinese brothers spent 20 years building their own Formula One racing car out of cooking pots, bicycles, and steel doors. Zhao Xiushun and Zhao Baoguo hand-built the car, which manages a top speed of 100 mph (160 km/h), entirely from materials they found on and around their farm in Tangshan.

TRUCK ROLL ■ Known as the "Human Speed Bump," Tom Owen from Birmingham, Alabama, allowed eight trucks—the last of which weighed 30,000 lb (13,607 kg)—to roll over his stomach at the 2008 Arizona State Fair. As the eighth truck passed over him, the ramps failed but although his lower body and legs were crushed beneath the wheels, five different X-rays showed that he hadn't broken a single bone. Owen has now been run over more than 1,000 times.

ECONOMY DRIVE ■ Australians John and Helen Taylor drove a Volkswagen 9,419 mi (15,158 km) through all 48 contiguous states of the United States in 20 days in 2008 and used only $653 worth of diesel, working out to about 6.9 cents per mile. They achieved an average 58.82 mi (94.66 km) to the gallon.

YOUNG MOZART ■ Talented pianist Curtis Bushell from London, England, has won a recording contract to perform Mozart—even though he is just four years old. He started learning the instrument at the age of three and in July 2008 he passed his grade-one piano exam after nine months of lessons. Within another three months, the little maestro had already reached grade-three standard.

STRIKING EYES ■ Ling Chunjiang of Kaifeng, China, can blow out candles with his eyes. By pinning his nose, he is able to blow air from his eyes through a hose and extinguish 12 candles in one minute. The martial arts enthusiast can also slice off the bottom of a beer bottle with his hand while keeping the rest of the bottle intact.

SOCCER JUGGLER ■ Graeme Lightbody from Johnstone, Scotland, juggled a soccer ball for an amazing six and a half hours in 2008 without letting the ball touch the ground once, achieving a total of 61,100 "keepie-uppies." To take in fluids during his marathon stint, he balanced the ball on his head. He maintained concentration by listening to an MP3 player of his favorite musical artists, including Tina Turner and Phil Collins.

SNAKE BOAT ■ In May 2008, boat makers in Kerala, India, launched a steel rowing boat that carried no fewer than 141 people. The snake boat—so called because the shape of the stern resembles the raised hood of a cobra—measured 143 x 6 ft (43.5 x 1.8 m) and weighed nearly nine tons.

CAN CREATION ■ Five architecture students from Montana State University created a huge sculpture from 45,725 cans of tuna fish and beans. The sculpture, which depicted a hand holding a can, measured a whopping 16 x 32 x 10 ft (5 x 10 x 3 m) and took a painstaking 41 hours to build.

FAMILY TREE ■ Roy Blackmore from Somerset, England, spent nearly 30 years tracing all his ancestors—and ended up creating a family tree that dated back 1,500 years and featured 9,390 of his relatives. His research, which covered around 45 generations, revealed him to be the great-grandson 37 times distant of King William the Conqueror, who invaded England from France in 1066.

HOP THE FENCE ■ Yo-yo expert Arron Sparks from London performed 144 "hop the fence" tricks in just one minute at an event in Suffolk, England, in July 2008—that's faster than two per second.

PILLOW FIGHT ■ No fewer than 3,872 fans took part in a mass pillow fight at the end of a Kane County Cougars baseball game at Geneva, Illinois, in July 2008.

TIGHT SQUEEZE ■ An attempt in August 2008 to see how many Texan cheerleaders could fit into an elevator together ended in panic when the elevator doors got stuck at the first floor. Even though signs clearly stated that the safety capacity was 15 people, 26 teenage girls had managed to squeeze into the confined space at the University of Texas in Austin, but they then had to wait 25 minutes before a repairman was able to release them.

DEAD MOSQUITOES ■ A Chinese man set up an online business in 2008 selling dead mosquitoes that he had killed personally. Nin Nan, of Shanghai, advertised them for around $1 a head, suggesting that the insect corpses could be used for scientific study, decoration, or collection. He had 10,000 orders in two days.

www.ripleybooks.com
>>>> go to >>>> @

WAUL BALL

Joel Waul of Lauderhill, Florida, has spent more than five years creating a huge ball from more than 700,000 rubber bands. The multicolored ball, which he calls Nugget, weighs around 9,000 lb (4,082 kg) and stands over 6 ft (1.8 m) high. He has already suffered for his art—when the ball was a mere 400 lb (181 kg), it rolled over his hand, spraining his wrist.

Toy Soldiers

An army of 35,310 LEGO® Star Wars figures stood guard at LEGO® headquarters in Slough, England, in June 2008. A group of employees spent a whole day assembling the miniature army—without use of "the force." The vast collection of Clone Troopers were the centerpiece of a charity event that helped celebrate the toy company's 50th birthday.

SOCK LINE ■ In July 2008, students at King Edward's School in Birmingham, England, created a washing line of socks that stretched for nearly a mile. They hung up more than 28,000 socks.

THUMBS UP ■ Using only his thumbs, Elliot Nicholls of Dunedin, New Zealand, can type a 160-character message into his cell phone in just 45 seconds—while blindfolded!

MODEL AUTOS ■ Suhail Mohammad Al Zarooni of Dubai, United Arab Emirates, has a collection of more than 7,000 miniature model autos, including models of the limo in which John F. Kennedy was shot, Hitler's Mercedes, and the cars driven by James Bond and Mr. Bean.

PENNY AUCTION ■ In February 2008, Walter Husak of Van Nuys, California, sold 301 antique pennies at an auction in Long Beach for $10.7 million. First place for value went to two coins dating back to the 18th century, which each sold for $632,500.

BANANAS BECKY ■ Becky Martz of Houston, Texas, is fascinated by bananas—not the fruits themselves but the labels. She began collecting banana labels in 1991 and now has more than 7,000. She has even started branching out to collect asparagus and broccoli bands.

FAST ROUND ■ In July 2008, more than 40 golfers representing a local radio station completed a round of golf at Boyne Falls, Michigan, in under eight minutes! Golfers were carefully placed on the course's tee boxes, along the fairways and on the greens. The timing started once the tee-shot was struck, with players on the fairway then running to hit the ball as it came to rest. Three holes were played six times in a row to achieve a total yardage of 6,096 (5,574 m).

PUZZLE SOLVED ■ Pensioner Eric Smith of Staffordshire, England, spent six months completing a 24,000-piece jigsaw puzzle. The 12 x 6 ft (3.6 x 1.8 m) picture of dolphins and boats took the retired sales manager 537 hours and was so big that he had to build a table to accommodate it and move it to his garage.

TUG-OF-WAR ■ More than 100,000 people took part in a tug-of-war contest in Lintan, China, in March 2007. To cope with the numbers, the "rope" was made of steel cables and at 5,850 ft (1,800 m) measured more than a mile long.

MIGHTY MUFFLER ■ Ray Ettinger of Independence, Missouri, spent nearly five years knitting a scarf that is 3,523 ft (1,074 m) long and weighs 75 lb (34 kg). His grandmother had taught him to knit when he was ten.

BOTTLE BANK ■ Since starting his collection in the mid-1970s, Tom Bates has amassed more than 36,000 beer and soda cans and 9,000 different bottles. They were displayed for a time at the Museum of Beverage Containers and Advertising in Millersville, Tennessee.

SKATER BOY ■ Chester Fried of South River, New Jersey, has visited every roller-skating rink across the United States—more than 300 in total. He put on his first pair of roller skates at age seven and now in his sixties owns more than 300 pairs.

BALANCING ACT ■ Nine-year-old Joe Allison of Devon, England, balanced 16 spoons on his face at the same time in April 2008. He balanced five on his forehead, one on each ear, two on his lips, four on his cheeks, two on his chin and one on his nose. Joe, who discovered his talent when his cousin challenged him to balance a spoon on his nose, is looking forward to growing so there is more space on his forehead.

HIGH RIDER ■ Nik Wallenda, the seventh generation of the Flying Wallendas circus family, walked along a high-wire suspended 135 ft (41 m) above the streets of Newark, New Jersey, and then cycled back along the wire—all without a safety net. He even made a cell-phone call halfway through the walk.

BOLLYWOOD EPIC ■ Ashish Sharma of Uttar Pradesh, India, watched 48 Bollywood movies for over 120 hours straight in June 2008.

FULL HOUSE ■ Jim Purol of Anaheim, California, sat in all 92,542 seats at the Pasadena Rose Bowl in five days in July 2008. Armed with a pad to cushion his backside against the plastic seats, and an umbrella-hat to shield his face from the sun, he sat for 12 hours each day and, despite the blisters he picked up along the way, he fulfilled the dream he had held for 20 years—ever since he sat in all 107,501 chairs at the University of Michigan's football stadium.

WEDDING VOWS ■ In February 2008, in Pittsburgh, Pennsylvania, 624 couples simultaneously renewed their wedding vows.

BRAINY HUG ■ Alan Baltis of Lakewood, Ohio, hugged 833 people in an hour at the Mensa annual conference in Denver, Colorado, in 2008—that's nearly 14 people a minute. Standing more than 6 ft (1.8 m) tall, he had to squat to complete many of the hugs.

MEDICAL DEVICES ■ Dr. Douglas Arbittier of New York collects old medical equipment. His collection includes amputation saws—some dating back to the 1730s—bloodletting artifacts, old stethoscopes, hearing devices, and dental instruments.

RED RALLY ■ In September 2008, some 2,000 redheads from 20 countries gathered in Breda, Holland, for a celebratory red-haired day.

Cram in the COCKROACHES

When Travis Fessler fancied a crunchy snack, he decided to pop 11 live Madagascar Hissing Cockroaches into his mouth at once. The insect fan from Kentucky intended to raise awareness for charity and said, "Madagascar Hissing Cockroaches don't bite or sting, but they do have tiny hooks on the ends of their legs that they use to help them climb. When used on the soft flesh of the inside of the mouth, it was a bit like Velcro rubbing on my tongue and cheeks." The creatures all survived Travis' mouth and now live in a terrarium in his house.

www.ripleybooks.com

12

Game of Squash

A basketball game between Dallas and Utah went from the tall to the small when a contortionist squeezed himself into a box in the half-time break in March 2006.

LOTTERY LOVER ■ Telecom engineer Victor Paul Taylor from Manchester, England, has been collecting scratchcards since 1995. He specializes in U.K. National Lottery scratchcards and could be sitting on a fortune because none of the cards have actually been scratched.

FIVE BRUSHES ■ At Changsha, China, in September 2008, Ye Genyou simultaneously used five brushes to write calligraphy on a piece of paper. He held two brushes in each hand and one in his mouth. He once wrote 7,659 characters on a piece of paper 330 ft (100 m) long and 31 in (80 cm) wide without lifting the brush for 17 hours 13 minutes.

GIANT JIGSAW ■ Some 15,000 jigsaw puzzle enthusiasts assembled a giant puzzle that almost covered the town square in Ravensburg, Germany. The 6,500-sq-ft (600-sq-m) puzzle consisted of 1,141,800 pieces and was put together in just five hours.

24-HOUR RELAY ■ Nearly 3,850 people took part in a 24-hour, 100-meter relay race in Riga, Latvia, in October 2008. The youngest competitor was a one-year-old toddler who walked the entire 110 yards (100 m) accompanied by his mom.

POOL CONTEST ■ At Spring Lake, North Carolina, in October 2008, Brian Lilley and Daniel Maloney played pool for 52 hours nonstop—completing more than 600 games.

BUILT COFFIN ■ Grady Hunter, 75, won a blue ribbon in the crafts and hobbies competition at the 2008 North Carolina State Fair—by making his own coffin. Hunter wanted to make the coffin more comfortable than most proprietary brands and he incorporated his signature into the wood.

EYES WRITE ■ A Chinese man can write calligraphy by shooting water from his eyes. Ru Anting from Luoyang, Henan Province, sucks up the water with his nose and then sprays it through his tear ducts onto a board covered with dark paper. He discovered his unusual talent as a child while swimming in a river and after three years of training, he can now shoot water accurately from his eyes over a distance of up to 10 ft (3 m).

TOMATO PASTE ■ Erik van de Wiel of the Netherlands collects tomato paste cans. He has hundreds in his collection, many sent to him by friends traveling in Europe and North America. Most of the cans are empty now because, if stored too long, they might eventually explode.

HUMAN TORCH ■ Dana Kunze from Minneapolis, Minnesota, dives from a height of 80 ft (24 m) into a pool—while on fire. Dressed in several layers of cotton shirts, pants, and hoods soaked with water, Kunze is doused with gasoline before being set on fire. He then delays his dive for up to 30 seconds, by which time he is feeling like toast!

COLD COMFORT ■ In 1996, four UPS workers from Calgary, Alberta, Canada, made a $400 bet to see who could go longest over the course of the year wearing shorts in his delivery job. In January 2008, as the temperature dropped to −50°F (−45°C) with wind chill, a winner finally emerged—Shaun Finnis who had happily worn shorts to work every day for more than 11 years, even in subfreezing weather.

HEAD CONTROL ■ Cuban women's soccer player Yeniseidis Soto managed to control a ball with her head for 2 hours 12 minutes 32 seconds in Havana in 2008—without it once touching the ground or any part of her body other than her head.

Human Flag

Daniel Ulizio from Midland, Pennsylvania, had the strength and sheer nerve to act as a human flag and "fly" from the top of a 100-ft (30-m) chimney in 1937.

Levitation Act

New Yorkers couldn't believe their eyes when Dutch magician Wouter Bijdendijk, also known as Ramana, levitated several feet above the ground in Times Square in October 2007, his only support apparently being a stick held in his left hand.

CONTINUOUS CHANT ■ Worshipers at the Shri Bala Hanuman temple in Jamnagar, India, have been chanting the name of Lord Hanuman continuously for more than 44 years. The chanting began on August 1, 1964, and by August 2008 it had been running for 16,070 days nonstop.

DAY-LONG SERMON ■ Rev. Eric Delve, the vicar of St. Luke's Church in Maidstone, Kent, England, gave a sermon lasting a full 24 hours in August 2008. His outdoor preaching marathon—reading passages from the Bible—was billed as "creation to the end of the world in 24 hours."

SAND CASTLE ■ More than 1,000 people helped creator Ed Jarrett build a sand castle that reached 31 ft 7 in (9.6 m) tall at Casco, Maine, in September 2007. Forty dump-loads of sand—weighing in at around 500 tons—went into building the castle.

CHAMPION BAGGER ■ Erika Jensen, a Macey's grocery-store employee from Utah, won the 2008 International Best Bagger Competition held in Las Vegas, Nevada, judged on her speed, weight distribution, and appearance. Three years earlier, her older sister Emily had won the title, and the 2007 champion bagger, Brian Bay, also came from Erika's store.

TWO-HANDED ■ Liam Doherty of Galway, Ireland, can write simultaneously with both hands, forward, backward, upside down, and mirror image.

MANY MOHAMMADS ■ More than 20,000 people—all named Mohammad—gathered simultaneously in the Libyan city of Zawia in July 2008. The participants included one man with six Mohammads in his own name. He is called Mohammad Mohammad Mohammad Mohammad Mohammad Mohammad Al Wish.

STRONG BOY ■ Seventeen-year-old Kye Thomas of Bristol, England, can lift loads of up to 476 lb (216 kg)—that's more than twice his bodyweight. The 210-lb (95 kg) boy—dubbed Superkid—won the title of Britain's Strongest Schoolboy in 2008 by picking up a 168-lb (76-kg) log seven times, flipping 700-lb (317-kg) truck tires and lugging 210-lb (95 kg) barrels across fields. He trains by partially lifting cars that are an incredible 15 times his body weight.

STARTING FROM SCRATCH ■ Gideon Weiss has a collection of more than 230 back scratchers. He has amassed his unusual treasures over the past ten years, and they include back scratchers from as far afield as Norway, Spain, and Thailand.

CALCULATING RUSSIAN ■ Sergei Frolov from St. Petersburg, Russia, has built up a collection of more than 150 Soviet-made calculators, as well as vintage computers, watches, and slide rules.

NECK DEEP ■ Mark McGowan spent 30 hours buried neck-deep in sand on the beach in Margate, Kent, England, in May 2008.

OREGON OREGAMI ■ Joseph Wiseman of Eugene, Oregon, folds paper airplanes that are just over ¼ in (7 mm) long—about the length of a grain of rice.

PRESSING BUSINESS ■ The owner of a dry-cleaning store, Ben Walton of Hampshire, England, ironed nonstop for 60 hours in July 2008, during which time he ironed 923 items—and suffered only a bad back.

PLANE SAILING ■ Motorcycle stuntman Doug Danger has jumped over a jumbo jet airplane. Danger from Palmer, Massachusetts, launched his bike from a narrow ramp at a speed of more than 70 mph (113 km/h) and sailed over the 160-ft (49-m) wingspan of the parked plane.

STRANGE SCORING ■ Scoring only three-point shots and foul shots, the Annandale (Minnesota) High School boys' basketball team amazingly won a game 51 points to 48 in February 2007.

SCIENCE DAY ■ To commemorate 2008 Science Day—a day set aside by school governors in Missouri, Illinois, and Tennessee to raise interest in science—children and adults managed to inflate 852 balloons in one hour at West Park Mall, Cape Girardeau, Missouri.

ELEPHANT MAN ■ Ed Gotwalt received his first ornamental elephant as a good-luck gift from his sister-in-law in 1967 and now has collected 6,000 elephant artifacts from all over the world and in every imaginable type of material. He keeps them at Mister Ed's Elephant Museum in Orrtanna, Pennsylvania, where visitors can marvel at an elephant potty chair, an elephant hair dryer, elephant lamps, and even an elephant pulling a 24-carat-gold circus wagon.

BIRTHDAY GREETINGS ■ James Bridges of Cadiz, Kentucky, has a contact list of more than 2,600 people—all of whom he calls on their birthday to sing "Happy Birthday."

FAST FEET ■ In November 2008, fleet-footed Martina Servaty created 11½ pt (5.4 l) of juice by furiously treading grapes for just one minute at Mesenich, Germany.

NAPKIN QUEEN ■ Helena Vnouckova from Prague, Czech Republic, has a collection of more than 16,000 napkins.

COIN TRICK ■ Tyler Johnson of Salisbury, Massachusetts, can drop 39 coins off his right elbow and catch them all in his right hand!

FAST TRACK ■ In 2008, Corey Pedersen from Montana and Californian Mike Kim traveled a total of 1,813 mi (2,901 km) on a series of high-speed Japanese trains in a 24-hour period.

GUITAR SESSION ■ Akash Gupta, age 14, played the guitar nonstop for 53 hours in Agra, India, in June 2008.

CUFF COLLECTOR ■ Joseph W. Lauher of New York collects vintage handcuffs. His collection, which also contains leg irons, nippers, and thumbcuffs, includes specimens from the United States, Europe, and the Far East.

DESERT RACES ■ Finishing in Morocco in March 2007, Sandy McCallum of Edmonton, Alberta, Canada, ran six desert ultramarathons—covering a total of 875 mi (1,408 km) in scorching heat—in the space of just 12 months.

Driving Dangerously

Liu Suozhu of Henan Province, China, performed a breathtaking stunt by driving a family car across two unsteady steel ropes that were suspended 150 ft (46 m) over the Minluo River in Pingjiang, in central China, in April 2008. It took Suozhu 30 minutes to complete the amazing 755-ft (230-m) journey.

NATIONAL FLAGS ■ Climbers from around the world—each carrying their national flag—scaled the Sydney Harbour Bridge in September 2008 and flew 137 flags from the summit of the Australian landmark. Each flag represented a country with a member who had joined BridgeClimb, an organization which, among other things, enables couples to exchange their wedding vows at the top of the bridge.

MOVIE SESSION ■ Suresh Joachim and Claudia Wavra sat through 123 continuous hours of movies—that's watching movies for more than five days—in New York City's Times Square in October 2008. They diligently watched 57 movies from the opening titles until the final credits rolled in each.

Hoopla!

A performer displays incredible hula-hooping skills during a cultural presentation in Beijing to celebrate Chinese New Year in February 2008.

Escape Artist

Escaping from a locked milk can 3 ft (0.9 m) high, bound by the feet in a water-filled torture cell with no air supply, Harry Houdini always made sure that his audience was shocked and thrilled.

Born in Hungary 1874, Houdini moved to the United States. when he was very young, and his dedication to the art of illusion soon made him one of the most famous names in the country. The original escape artist inspired countless imitators but always stayed one step ahead by copyrighting his pioneering illusions and continually inventing new tricks. These included being buried alive on stage and swallowing needles and thread. Houdini would escape from the coffin in less than two minutes, and regurgitated the needles one by one, each threaded with cotton.

Houdini's most vital skill was escaping from handcuffs and picking locks; he offered rewards to anyone who could provide cuffs or ropes he could not escape from. In 1904, a London newspaper produced a unique pair of cuffs that had taken five years to make, yet Houdini still wriggled free. In more than 30 years of performing, he never had to pay a challenger.

The daredevil magician defied death on hundreds of occasions and it was not his famous escapes that killed him. Houdini was renowned for his resistance to pain, and in 1926 an over-zealous member of the public asked to punch him in the stomach to test his strength. Houdini was caught unprepared and, wanting to continue with performing, he didn't seek medical attention for days. Tragically, he had been suffering from appendicitis when he'd been hit and he never recovered.

Water Torture

In 1912, Houdini unveiled his most daring escape yet. Secured by the feet inside a watertight chamber, he would escape within minutes. Such was the force required that he once broke his ankle in escaping. Although Houdini requested that the cell be burned upon his death, his brother kept it intact. The magician got his wish, however, as a museum fire destroyed the torture cell in 1995.

Extraordinaire

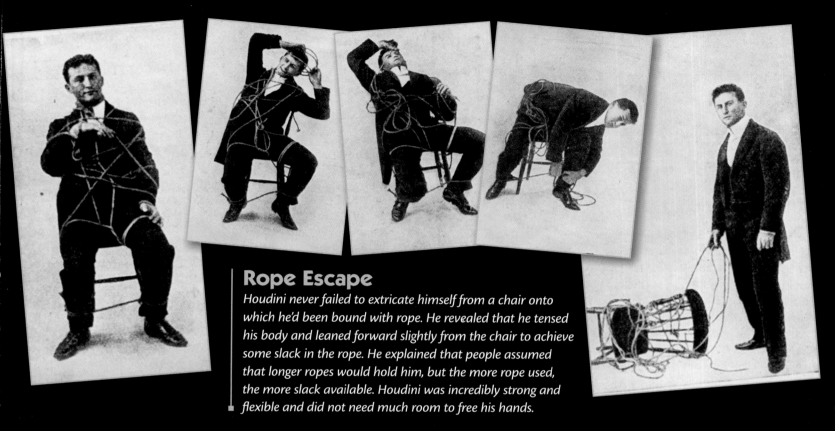

Rope Escape

Houdini never failed to extricate himself from a chair onto which he'd been bound with rope. He revealed that he tensed his body and leaned forward slightly from the chair to achieve some slack in the rope. He explained that people assumed that longer ropes would hold him, but the more rope used, the more slack available. Houdini was incredibly strong and flexible and did not need much room to free his hands.

HOUDINI'S STUNTS

> Locked inside a water-torture cell

> Escape from a locked milk can full of water

> Suspended from a building in a straitjacket

> Handcuffed inside a nailed-shut packing crate, and thrown in a river

> Escape from a jail cell

> Swallowing needles and thread

> Buried alive on stage

> Escape from any pair of handcuffs

Milk Can Escape

One of Houdini's most famous performances was the escape from a locked milk can full of water. He would be hidden behind a curtain, and emerge drenched in water.

BURNING RUBBER

www.ripleybooks.com

The motorsport of Gymkhana requires drivers to drift sideways around seemingly impossible corners and spin through circles at breakneck speeds on a specially laid-out track. Expert stunt driver Ken Block is so adept at controlling his car that he can slide 360 degrees sideways round a moving target, such as a Segway scooter and its brave rider.

ROCKET MAN ■ Swiss adventurer Yves Rossy flew 22 mi (35 km) across the English Channel in 2008 with only a home-made rocket-powered wing strapped to his back. After Rossy was dropped from a plane 8,000 ft (2,440 m) above the French coast, the power from the four mini-jets attached to the 8-ft (2.4-m) carbon-fiber wing enabled him to make the crossing in less than 10 minutes at speeds of more than 125 mph (200 km/h). As his lightweight wing had no steering mechanism, he had to use his head and back to control the wing's movement.

BOXING VETERAN ■ Saoul Mamby of New York City is 60 years old and still boxes professionally against anyone in his weight class—no matter how old they are.

DIRT BUSTER ■ Twelve-year-old Kyle Krichbaum of Adrian, Michigan, has a collection of 165 vacuum cleaners and he vacuums his house five times a day. He got his first vacuum at age one, he dressed up as a Dirt Devil for Halloween at age two, and by age six, instead of going outside during school recesses, he often stayed indoors to vacuum the principal's office.

CHESS CHAMP ■ Twelve-year-old Peter Williams from Hampshire, England, has been playing chess since the age of five—and now he is so good that he can beat opponents even while blindfolded!

BREATHTAKING BLAINE ■ Brooklyn-born magician David Blaine managed to hold his breath underwater for more than 17 minutes on an April 2008 edition of *The Oprah Winfrey Show*. After inhaling pure oxygen to flush carbon dioxide from his blood, Blaine, wearing a silver wetsuit, was lowered into a sphere containing around 1,800 gallons of water. He had hoped to stay underwater for longer, but became aware that his heart was beating irregularly toward the end of the stunt.

WORD MEMORY ■ Listening just once to 140 random words, 18-year-old Rajiv Sharma, from Sarlahi, Nepal, was able to repeat 119 of them in ten minutes.

MARATHON WOMAN ■ In July 2008, Pauline Newsholme from Devon, England, ran her 69th marathon—at the age of 69.

HIGH TEE ■ Golf fanatic Andrew Winfield from Northampton, England, teed off from the summit of Africa's Mount Kilimanjaro in 2008—19,340 ft (5,895 m) above sea level. The 50-year-old climbed for a week with his specially adapted collapsible six-iron, before hitting his high tee shot.

GLOBAL TRAVELER ■ In May 2008, Kashi Samaddar, a Dubai-based Indian businessman, completed his quest to visit all of the world's 194 sovereign states—a journey that took him four-and-a-half years. The first country he visited was Uruguay and the last was the Serbian province of Kosovo.

DOMINO TOPPLING ■ In November 2008, 85 people from 13 countries gathered in the Netherlands to set up and knock over a chain of 4,354,027 domino blocks.

CARP CATCH ■ Forty-one teams of paired fishermen caught more than 18 tons of carp in 50 hours during the American Carp Society's 2008 Northeast Tournament in Baldwinsville, New York.

Skateboard Journey

New Zealander Rob Thomson embarked on the trip of a lifetime when he traveled 7,500 mi (12,000 km) on a skateboard. The trip lasted 462 days, and took him from Switzerland to Shanghai via Europe and the United States. He even journeyed the entire length of China. Rob traveled solo and unsupported, carrying all his belongings on the specially modified skateboard trailer.

WHEELBARROW PUSH ■ David Baird, a 65-year-old British man, pushed a wheelbarrow 2,572 mi (4,139 km) across Australia in 112 days. He set off from Perth in September 2008 and reached Sydney in January 2009, having pushed between 10 and 12 hours a day.

VETERAN BODYBUILDER ■ Ray Moon of Thornbury, Victoria, Australia, has won four state and national bodybuilding competitions—at age 80. He began bodybuilding only in 2004 and does five fitness sessions a week, each consisting of 2.5 mi (4 km) on a treadmill and 45 minutes of weight training.

JET SKI ■ In January 2009, Roy Ogletree of Columbus, Ohio, traveled 1,080 mi (1,738 km) in 24 hours on a jet ski on Lake Lloyd in the infield of the Daytona Beach International Speedway.

Flying Feet

Jessica Cox from Tucson, Arizona, is one of a kind, being the first woman without arms to receive a pilot's license. Already able to drive a car, the motivational speaker was born without arms and prefers not to use prosthetic limbs, instead performing regular tasks with her feet.

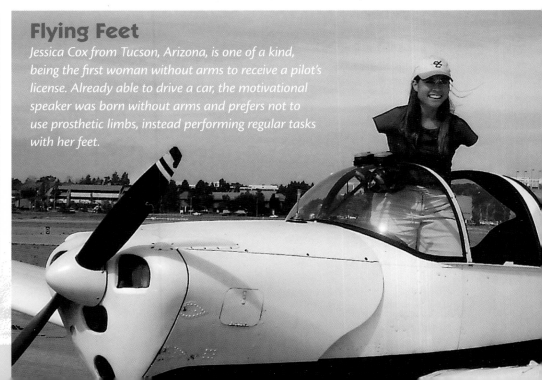

PEAK FITNESS ■ In 2007, 76-year-old Michio Kumamoto from Tokorozawa, Japan, climbed Alaska's 20,320-ft-high (6,194-m) Mount McKinley, which is the tallest peak in North America.

COIN HOARDER ■ After begging on the streets of Calcutta for 44 years, Laxmi Das has finally saved up enough money—around $700—to open her own bank account and even qualify for a credit card. She had collected thousands of coins—weighing a total of 200 lb (90 kg)—in iron buckets at her shanty-town home.

LONG WALK HOME ■ On October 3, 2007, 231,635 Canadians walked 1.6 mi (1 km) at more than 1,000 different venues.

SEVEN CONTINENTS ■ At just ten years old, Victoria White of Elizabeth, Colorado, completed a mission to ski on all seven continents. She and her father Ken spent a year traveling 75,000 mi (120,700 km) by air and 3,500 mi (5,630 km) by sea, finishing their journey at Winter Park, Colorado, in March 2008.

FAMILY FORTUNE ■ In 2007, the Leblanc family of Moncton, New Brunswick, Canada, had 13 living siblings ranging in age from 71 to 88.

LONG TOUR ■ In June 2003, 21 tourists spent more than 33 hours on a guided tour of the German city of Augsburg, listening to nearly 100 city guides who worked in shifts.

STREET WALKER ■ David Marsh walks 18 mi (29 km) a day in his job cleaning the streets of Wigan, England, which means that in his 40-year career Marsh, who has never had a sick day, has clocked up more than 169,000 mi (272,000 km)—the equivalent of walking around the world six times.

ROOKIE COP ■ Laurence Egerton became a rookie cop in 2007—at age 56. The former businessman joined the Wilmington Police Department in North Carolina.

CHIPPER GRAN ■ A great-grandmother celebrated her 100th birthday in 2007 by frying fish and chips in her shop. Connie Brown still works six days a week at the fish-and-chip shop in Pembroke, Wales, that she opened in 1928 with her late husband Sidney.

BLISTERING BATTLE ■ In 2006, 3,745 people enjoyed a snowball fight in Houghton, Michigan.

BRAVE SOLDIER ■ A British soldier serving in southern Afghanistan in 2008 threw himself onto an exploding grenade to save the lives of his patrol—and walked away with nothing worse than a bloody nose. Royal Marine lance corporal Matt Croucher from Birmingham survived the blast because his knapsack took most of the force of the explosion.

REAL FL-AIR ■ In 2005, 4,083 air guitarists mimed to "Sweet Child of Mine" by Guns N' Roses in Guildford, England.

HO, HO, HO! ■ In Derry, Northern Ireland, in 2007, 12,965 people dressed as Santa Claus.

DANCING COP ■ On the streets of Provincetown, Massachusetts, police officer Donald Thomas has been directing traffic with exaggerated dance movements for more than 50 years—and he was still going strong in 2008 at the age of 81.

HARMONIOUS TUNE ■ In 2005, 1,706 harmonica players performed "Twinkle, Twinkle, Little Star" in Seattle, Washington.

SAME SURNAME ■ A total of 1,488 people with the surname Gallagher gathered at Letterkenny, County Donegal, Ireland, in 2007.

DOUBLE ACHIEVEMENT ■ Jeanne Stawiecki from Charlton, Massachusetts, has run marathons on all seven continents and climbed the "Seven Summits," the highest mountain on each continent—a feat all-the-more remarkable because she did not even start mountain climbing until she was 52.

COLLABORATIVE CEREMONY ■ In 2007, 3,500 priests took part in a single religious ceremony at Jaipur, India.

LIFE OR DEATH ■ Residents of Taipei, Taiwan, simultaneously administered mouth-to-mouth resuscitation in 2007— 3,429 of them!

SUPER-SIZED SKETCH ■ In 2006, 3,000 people helped draw a teapot on a giant Etch A Sketch® in Boston, Massachusetts.

FARMING FRENZY ■ At Cooley, County Louth, Ireland, in 2007, 4,572 tractor drivers plowed a field simultaneously.

RELENTLESS RALLY ■ Andrea Holt played a nonstop table tennis rally with Alex Perry and Mark Roscaleer for 8 hours 27 minutes in Manchester, England, in 2007.

TIGER CUB ■ In 2007, an English golfer hit his third hole-in-one—and he was still only eight years old. David Huggins from Stowmarket, Suffolk, hit his first ace when he was four—two years younger than when Tiger Woods struck his first hole-in-one.

FLYING HIGH ■ An amazing 18,000 people created a human depiction of the Portuguese national flag in Lisbon in 2006.

BIG HUG ■ A big group hug took place in 2008 when 12,000 students from Ottawa, Ontario, Canada, embraced.

WHAT A SCARE ■ In 2008, there were 5,441 scarecrows present in the town of Hoschton, Georgia, U.S.A.

SUPER SMOOCH ■ In 2007, 7,451 couples kissed simultaneously in Budapest, Hungary.

STILL STANDING ■ Suresh Joachim balanced on one foot for 76 hours in Sri Lanka in 1997.

TV ADDICT ■ Chris Dean and Mike Dudek of Grand Rapids, Michigan, watched TV nonstop for 52 hours in 2004.

CHECK MATE ■ In Mexico City's Zocalo Square in 2006, 13,446 people played games of chess simultaneously.

HOCKEY MARATHON ■ Mike Nabuurs played air hockey for 48 hours in Hamilton, Ontario, in 2005.

FULL HOUSE ■ At the Canadian National Exhibition in 1983, 15,756 players took part in a single game of bingo.

TWO-DAY TENNIS ■ Brian Jahrsdoerfer, Michel Lavoie, Peter Okpokpo, and Warner Tse played doubles tennis for 48 hours in Houston, Texas, in 2006.

RING THE BELLS ■ Joe Defries of Abbotsford, British Columbia, played the handbells for 28 hours in 2005.

DRIBBLED BALL ■ Joseph Odhiambo from Phoenix, Arizona, dribbled a basketball for 26 hours through the streets of Houston, Texas, in 2006.

SPINNING SUCCESS ■ Ashrita Furman of New York managed to spin a top for 7 hours 1 minute in 2006.

WINNING PIERCINGS

To celebrate the 2008 Olympic Games in Beijing, a Chinese man, Dr. Wei Sheng, pierced his head, face, hands, and chest in the five colors of the Olympic rings with 2,008 needles.

SCORPION QUEEN ■ In December 2008, Thailand's "Scorpion Queen," Kanchana Kaetkaew, held a venomous scorpion in her mouth for more than two minutes. She allowed her husband to place the live scorpion on her tongue, where it remained for 2 minutes 3 seconds before she spat it out.

EIGHT-HOUR SPEECH ■ An Australian politician made an eight-hour speech to delay a vote on changes to workers' compensation laws. Mark Parnell, a member of South Australia's Greens party, started his speech at 11a.m. on May 8, 2008, and finished 12 hours later, having paused only for lunch and dinner.

MASKED MAN ■ Gerold Weschenmoser of Germany has over 5,000 masks in a collection that he started more than 50 years ago, in 1957.

AGILE FEET ■ Anssi Vanhala of Finland can solve a Rubik's Cube puzzle in less than 40 seconds using only his feet.

MATCHSTICK SHUTTLE

Ken Applegate from St. Petersburg, Florida, spent 12 years making a 1:10 scale replica of the *Challenger* space shuttle from over half a million matchsticks. More than 12 ft (3.6 m) long and weighing about 800 lb (365 kg), the matchstick model was completed in 2008 and even has moving features, including opening cargo bay doors and retractable wheels.

26-HOUR GAME ■ Twenty-four members of Havering Field Hockey Club in Essex, England, played indoor hockey for 26 hours nonstop in December 2008.

HAND WALKER ■ At the age of 96, Fred Birchmore of Athens, Georgia, kept fit by walking 3 mi (4.8 km) every day, going swimming—and walking on his hands. In his youth, he once cycled around the world.

SNAKE EATER ■ Wen Xide from Zhumadian, China, enjoys eating live snakes and washing them down with a bottle of beer. He started eating snakes more than ten years ago to win a bet with friends and soon became addicted to them, even though he describes the experience as "a bit smelly." His son is now following in his footsteps and devoured eight live snakes in 2008.

TRACTOR WHEELIE ■ In July 2008, Mike Hagan of Whitehall, Montana, drove his 1994 Ford tractor for a distance of 5.3 mi (8.5 km) on just its two rear wheels. His endurance wheelie lasted 35 minutes.

LEGO® LOVER ■ Darren Smith of Exeter, Devon, England, started collecting LEGO® bricks when he was five—and now, 28 years later, he has more than two million of them. His collection fills his large garage and a specially converted loft, and even threatens to spill over into the rest of the house. His wife Claire says: "If Darren had his way, we'd have a LEGO® extension built."

LEI LINE ■ In May 2008, volunteers in Waikiki, Hawaii, strung together flowers to form a lei (flower garland) that measured over a mile (1.6 km) long.

SEAT FEAT ■ Just weeks after undergoing a triple hernia operation, Terry Twining from Hampshire, England, sat on 40,040 seats at Belgium's national soccer stadium in 48 hours— an average of one seat every four seconds.

BAND-AID® TINS ■ Kevin Savetz from Blue Lake, California, has a collection of Band-Aid® tins. The idea for the collection started in 1994 when he found two dozen Band-Aid® tins dating back to the 1950s in the garage of the house he had just bought.

BALL GAME ■ Organized by Rick Thistle, 40 participants—male and female—played a softball game that lasted a staggering 96 hours 4 minutes in Charlottetown, Prince Edward Island, Canada, in 2008. The marathon game comprised 467 innings and 1,941 runs.

UNDERWATER CYCLIST ■ Helped onto his bike by local scuba divers, 62-year-old Italian Vittorio Innocente cycled underwater at a depth of 213 ft (65 m) in the sea near Genoa, Italy, in July 2008.

REVERSE SKATING ■ Rafael Mittenzwei roller-skated more than 130 mi (209 km) in 24 hours in August 2008—backward. He completed 685 laps of the track in Gross-Gerau, Germany, skating right through the night.

RUNNING BACKWARD ■ Xu Zhenjun of China ran a marathon in 3 hours 43 minutes 39 seconds—while facing backward!

PUB CRAWL ■ Since 1984, four men from West Bromwich, England, have visited more than 14,000 pubs across the U.K. and the Republic of Ireland. In that time, Peter Hill, John Drew, Karl Bradley, and Joe Hill have each drunk around 21,000 pints of beer.

HIGH JUMP ■ To mark the start of 2009, Australian stunt motorcyclist Robbie Maddison sped up a ramp in Las Vegas, Nevada, and catapulted 120 ft (37 m) through the air to land on top of a 100-ft-high (30-m) replica of the Arc de Triomphe.

YOUNG BUSINESSMAN ■ While being treated for leukemia, 10-year-old Brandon Rayner of Phoenix, Arizona, has collected more than 900,000 business cards.

Beads Galore

British artist and jeweler Alayna Slater used 10,000 multicolored beads to create a 262-ft-long (80-m) bracelet. It took Alanya 40 hours to make the incredible piece while she was at a fashion show in Birmingham, England, in 2008.

Spinning Around

Escape artist Rick Meisel needed all his unique talents when he was locked in a spinning washing machine full of soapsuds in September 2008. Incredibly, he survived long enough to free himself from six pairs of handcuffs and two leg irons before extricating his body from the tiny drum. The space inside was so small that the daredevil had himself surgically altered so that he could fit in it.

FEELING THE PINCH ■ Mark Billington, an eight-year-old boy from Braidwood, New South Wales, Australia, managed to clip 64 clothespins to his head.

LONG SMOKE ■ In Havana, Cuba, in May 2008, José Castelar Cairo hand-rolled a cigar that was nearly 150 ft (45 m) in length—that's longer than four buses standing nose-to-tail.

HAIR-RAISING ■ In May 2008, Shailendra Roy of India pulled a train engine and three coaches—a combined weight of more than 40 tons—using only his hair, braided into a ponytail. Roy, who has also pulled cars, trucks, logs, and buses by the same method, keeps his hair strong by rubbing it with mustard oil.

NOSE WHISTLER ■ Brandon Baugh of Tampa, Florida, can whistle "The Star-Spangled Banner"— through his nose. He discovered his unusual talent at school when, taking a deep breath one day, he heard a whistle coming from his nostrils. After a little practice, he found he could nose-whistle at will and now boasts an extensive repertoire of tunes.

BOUND TO SUCCEED ■ In April 2008, friends and fitness fanatics Heather Derbyshire and Karen Fingerhut ran up 54 flights of stairs with two of their legs tied together—in under 15 minutes. The pair ascended the 1,188 stairs of the winding fire escape of the UK's tallest building—London's Canary Wharf Tower—in 14 minutes 34.69 seconds.

SHOE DRIVE ■ No fewer than 10,512 shoes were displayed at the National Geographic Society in Washington, D.C., in July 2008, in a chain of footwear stretching 1.65 mi (2.65 km). Among the contributors was eight-year-old Peter Wajda from Mount Laurel, New Jersey, who organized a shoe drive and collected 509.

COUCH POTATO ■ Manhattan librarian Stan Friedman started 2008 by watching sports on TV for 29 hours continuously. He won a New Year's couch potato contest staged by a restaurant in Times Square, New York City. Four contestants sat in recliners and watched sports with unlimited food and drink, but they weren't allowed to sleep and could take a bathroom break only every eight hours. Friedman took home $5,000 in prizes, including a TV, a recliner, and a trophy adorned with a potato.

ETERNAL TRIANGLE ■ In May 2008, students and math teachers at Ironton High School, Ohio, built a paper tower 10 ft (3 m) tall, consisting of 16,384 tetrahedrons. They spent a month cutting out thousands of triangles from construction paper, decorating them and taping them together.

TEEN TEXTER ■ Drew Acklin, 17, from Cleveland, Ohio, sent or received 19,678 text messages in just 30 days in 2008. On average, he handled a text every two minutes during his waking hours over the entire month.

PENNY CHAIN ■ In July 2008, hundreds of volunteers in Fort Scott, Kansas, worked for three days to lay a chain of pennies that stretched for an incredible 40 mi (64 km) in a school parking lot. The line consisted of 3,406,234 coins.

HIGH HEELS ■ Thirty-eight-year-old Jill Stamison of Grand Haven, Michigan, ran a 150-m (164-yd) sprint in 21.95 seconds in New York's Central Park in July 2008—while wearing 3-in (7.6-cm) high heels.

SMURF GATHERING ■ More than 1,200 people descended on Castleblayney, Ireland, on July 18, 2008—to dress up as Smurfs. The participants wore blue and white clothes and any visible skin was painted blue with colored greasepaint.

BOUNCING BOYS ■ Operating in shifts of two people at a time, eight boys, aged between 8 and 11, bounced nonstop for 24 hours on an inflatable castle in Flat Rock, Michigan, in August 2008.

RUBBER BANDS ■ After two years spent collecting rubber bands, Étienne Anglehart of Montreal, Quebec, Canada, had so many that, when they were placed end to end in 2008, they stretched for about 12 mi (19 km). For easy transportation, he keeps them in 19 rolls—each the size of a basketball.

MILLION POSTMARKS ■ The Post Mark Museum in Bellevue, Ohio, houses examples of more than a million different postmarks collected from around the world.

RUM LABELS ■ Petr Hlousek from Prague, Czech Republic, has collected more than 6,600 rum bottle labels from 98 different countries.

A–Z OF CHOCOLATE ■ Martin Mihál of Germany has been collecting empty chocolate wrappers from around the world since 1996. He has almost 40,000 wrappers from approximately 100 different countries—everywhere from Andorra to Zimbabwe.

TRASH MISER ■ To determine how much waste he creates over a 12-month period, Ari Derfel of Berkeley, California, saved every piece of his non-food garbage throughout 2007, right down to tissues, drinking straws, and receipts. Friends were ordered not to give him any gifts, especially bottles of wine or anything in wrapping paper, but he still managed to accumulate 96 cubic ft (2.7 cubic m) of garbage in his house.

WALL OF FIRE ■ At an air show in Terre Haute, Indiana, in 2007, a crew of 35 people used more than 2,000 gal (7,570 l) of gasoline to create an instant wall of fire that was 6,637 ft (2,023 m) long.

ANGEL DISPLAY ■ Joyce Berg of Beloit, Wisconsin, has collected around 13,000 angels since 1976. Her collection, which is displayed in a local museum, includes angels made from cornhusks and spaghetti, angels adorning bells, music boxes and banks, and angels depicting everything from musicians to sports figures and Biblical to cartoon characters. Joyce loves angels so much that she has even been known to don wings and a halo to greet visitors.

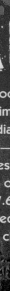

MELON HEAD

The brother of sharpshooter John Richmond truly trusts him with his life. John, from Granger, Indiana, claims to have shot—and missed—his brother Ken more than 100 times. He blew a watermelon off the top of Ken's head with a rifle from 25 ft (7.6 m) and has also successfully targeted objects placed on his brother's chest and face.

COCONUT CRAZY

Andres Gardin from Panama performs incredible feats of a dental nature. He has an appetite for coconuts, but not the milk inside—in Panama City in 2007, Gardin peeled the fibers off 500 coconuts in six hours using only his teeth.

FAMILY RIDE ■ Three generations of a Welsh family cycled across the United States. from Cape Canaveral, Florida, to San Diego, California, in 60 days. Nine-year-old Ann Lintern accompanied her mother Julie Smith on a tandem while 62-year-old grandfather Victor cycled behind them during the 3,260-mi (5,245-km) journey.

KING RAT ■ Impoverished Bangladeshi farmer Binoy Kumar Karmakar won a color T.V. set after killing 39,650 rats during 2008. He was crowned the country's rat-killing champion after displaying the collection of his victims' tails to government officials.

PLASTIC WRAP ■ Seven-year-old Jake Lonsway from Bangor Township, Michigan, created a plastic-wrap ball that was so big he could barely see over the top of it! The ball, which had a circumference of 138 in (3.5 m) and weighed about 281 lb (127 kg), took Jake eight months to build in the garage of the family home.

TRIPLE TREAT ■ Playing in a baseball game for Portsmouth High School, Ohio, in May 2008, triplets Howard, John, and Matt Harcha all hit home runs—in the order of their birth from oldest to youngest.

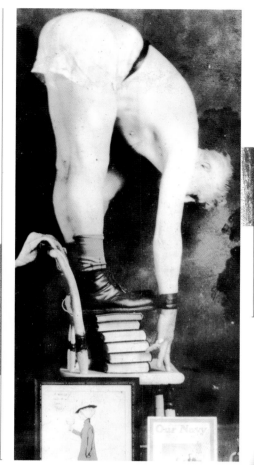

Stretchy Senior

In 1934, W.M. Keefe from New London, Connecticut, was able to touch his toes and then reach down a further 10 in (25 cm), despite being 73 years old.

SUPER SURFER ■ Rico de Souza rode a 30-ft-long (9-m), 224-lb (102-kg) surfboard for ten seconds off the coast of Rio de Janeiro, Brazil, in 2008.

GIRL PITCHER ■ A team in the Kansai Independent Baseball League in Japan drafted 16-year-old high school student Eri Yoshida, making her the country's first female professional pitcher to play alongside men.

Amazing Eyelids

Kung fu master Dong Changsheng from Changchun, China, attached hooks to his eyelids and pulled a 3,748-lb (1,700-kg) minibus carrying two adult men along the road. Dong has 35 years' experience in martial arts and achieves his extreme endeavors with the help of special breathing exercises.

CHAIR FLIP

Aaron Fotheringham from Las Vegas, Nevada, can perform a back flip in a wheelchair. Aaron, who was born with spina bifida and has been almost permanently confined to a wheelchair since the age of eight, spends more than 30 hours a week at the skate park, using a specially adapted aluminum wheelchair with suspension and grind bars to help him perform his amazing stunts.

FIVE-YEAR RUN ■ In 2008, a British grandmother completed a five-year run around the world. Pulling her supplies in a cart, Rosie Swale-Pope from Tenby, Wales, survived freezing temperatures in Alaska, was hit by a bus in Siberia, came face to face with a polar bear in Greenland, suffered pneumonia and frostbite, was nearly swept to her death in a raging river, and received 29 marriage proposals.

FAST DRIVE ■ Joshua Keeler, Joey Stocking, and Adam Gatherum of North Salt Lake, Utah, traveled more than 7,000 mi (11,265 km) by road through each of the 48 states in the continental United States in 2008, completing the journey in just 106 hours and 43 minutes.

STREET CLEANER ■ Ding Youzhen of Dongtai City, China, cleans the streets around her home every day—even though she is 104. She has been tidying up the city's streets for free for more than 84 years.

FREE RIDE ■ Kris Mole from Southwick, Sussex, visited 26 capital cities on a six-month, 9,763-mi (15,712-km) trek around Europe without spending a penny. Instead, he begged rides, went days without food, and slept outdoors when not offered a bed for the night.

OLD-TIMER ■ A 90-year-old D.J. announced her retirement in 2007 after 37 years at the turntable. Margaret Brelsford—or D.J. Master Maggie to her friends—played old-time dance music at Platt Social Club in Accrington, England.

JUNIOR LINGUIST ■ By the age of three, Seth Kinast of Hutchinson, Kansas, could recite the alphabet in Greek, count in German and Spanish, and had read almost 1,200 books.

GOLF BRAWL ■ A Florida golfer chose a four-iron to fight off an 11-ft-long (3.3-m) alligator as it attacked a diver who was looking for lost balls in a lake. Matt Johnson used the club and a rake to hit the reptile on the head as it grappled with unsuspecting diver Dwight Monreal at the Tampa Palms Golf and Country Club in April 2008.

GOLFING ACE ■ A 92-year-old blind golfer hit a hole-in-one in Florida in 2008. Leo Fiyalko, who needs help lining up his shots, struck the ace—his first-ever—while playing a 110-yd (100-m) hole in Clearwater.

MOWER RIDE ■ Accompanied by his dog Yoda, Paul Woods of Mystic, Connecticut, completed a 6,000-mi (9,660-km) trip from Alaska to Connecticut riding on a lawn mower. With the machine having a top speed of just 15 mph (24 km/h), the journey took him more than a year and a half.

MEMORY MAN ■ Despite being diagnosed with attention deficit hyperactivity disorder and dyslexia in high school, Dave Farrow from Toronto, Ontario, Canada, can memorize the exact order of 59 decks of playing cards all shuffled together— that's recalling 3,068 cards in order!

BIKE RIDE ■ Mark Beaumont from Fife, Scotland, cycled 18,000 mi (29,000 km) around the world in 195 days. He traveled through 20 countries, braving floods, robbers and being knocked off his bike in Louisiana when an elderly motorist ran a red light.

RIVER SWIM ■ In 2008, 21-year-old Katie Spotz of Mentor, Ohio, completed a 326-mi (525-km) swim of Pennsylvania's Allegheny River in a month. She swam for up to eight hours a day and on her best day covered 22 mi (35 km).

LOFTY AMBITION ■ Neil Sauter completed an eight-week, 835-mi (1,354-km) journey across Michigan in 2008—on aluminum stilts.

HOT SHOT ■ Randy Oitker of Plainville, Illinois, once hit five coin-sized targets with five arrows fired simultaneously from his bow.

EPIC WALK ■ Rick Wallenda, a descendant of the famous "Flying Wallendas" circus troupe, walked 2,000 ft (610 m) along a tightrope just $5/8$ in (1.5 cm) wide, suspended 112 ft (34 m) above ground at Kings Island, Mason, Ohio, on July 4, 2008. Without safety nets or harnesses and using a 38-lb (17-kg) pole to maintain his balance, he completed the walk in 35 minutes.

PERFECT GAME ■ A 78-year-old blind man bowled 12 back-to-back strikes to record his first-ever perfect game at the Century Lanes bowling alley in Alta, Iowa. Dale Davis had given up his love for the sport after losing his sight to macular degeneration but, encouraged by his sister, he now plays six games a week even though he can't see the lane or the pins.

EVER PRESENT ■ Andria Baker of Constantine, Michigan, didn't miss a day of school from kindergarten all the way through 12th grade.

HAPPY EVER AFTER ■ Indian couple 103-year-old Pyara Singh and 101-year-old Hansa Devi celebrated their 83rd wedding anniversary in May 2007. They attribute their happy life together to disciplined living, controlled diet, and honesty.

AGED RAPPELLER ■ Partially blind Eve Mobbs from West Sussex, England, rappelled down the outside of a multistory parking garage in 2008—at 92 years of age.

FLYING HIGH ■ Bob Brown from Nottinghamshire, England, was still pole-vaulting in his seventies. In 2007, he was selected to compete in the British Athletics League against vaulters less than a quarter his age.

BLIND CLIMBER ■ Even though he has been blind since the age of five, John Wimmer of Medford, Oregon, has conquered more than half a dozen mountains across the United States. In the summer of 2008, accompanied by his guide dog Rasha and friend Diego Joven, Wimmer climbed 11,249 ft (3,429 m) to the summit of Mount Hood, Oregon.

MALL MARATHON ■ Boyd Otero of Zanesville, Ohio, has walked 20,000 laps— 10,000 mi (16,000 km)—around his local mall in less than five years.

BACKWARD WALK ■ For five months in 2007, Bill Kathan Jr., 55, of Vernon, Vermont, walked across the United States—backward. He set off from Concord, New Hampshire, in April and completed his 3,330-mi (5,360-km) reverse march in Newport, Oregon, in September.

Human Spider

Known as "Spider-Man" for his death-defying exploits in scaling the outsides of buildings all over the world using only his bare hands and climbing shoes, Frenchman Alain Robert climbed Paris's 625-ft-high (190-m) Tour Total for the sixth time in 2008. Over the past 20 years, he has climbed more than 80 skyscrapers and monuments, including the 1,483-ft-high (452-m) Petronas Twin Towers in Kuala Lumpur, Malaysia, and New York's 1,250-ft (381-m) Empire State Building.

SERIAL JUMPER ■ Martin Downs from Yorkshire, England, skydived on six continents in eight days in August 2008. He started with a 10,000-ft (3,050-m) jump in Natal, South Africa, before moving on to Madrid in Spain, Caracas in Venezuela, Los Angeles in the United States, Sydney in Australia, and Nhathang in Vietnam.

WONDER SHOT ■ A 74-year-old grandmother achieved a one-in-a-million archery shot by splitting one arrow with another – even though she is blind. Tilly Trotter from Devon, England, has been an archer for only two years and although she can see movement, she has no central vision, instead relying on her husband to tell her how near her shots are to the target.

TOY CATCH ■ After a 25-minute struggle, David Hayes from Wilkes County, North Carolina, caught a sizeable 21-lb (9.5-kg) catfish in 2008—with his three-year-old granddaughter Alyssa's Barbie fishing rod. At 32 in (81 cm) in length, the fish was 2 in (5 cm) longer than the pink plastic rod.

HUMAN CALCULATOR ■ Alexis Lemaire, a student at Reims University, France, worked out the 13th root of a random 200-digit number in his head in just 70 seconds in 2007. His answer of 2407899893032210 was the only correct solution from a possible 393 trillion combinations. He discovered his talent at age nine and began solving the roots of 200-digit numbers after finding that 100-digit numbers were too easy.

SEVEN MARATHONS ■ A blind British runner completed seven marathons on seven continents in seven days in April 2008. Dave Heeley, 50, from West Bromwich, ran a total of 183 mi (295 km) in the Falkland Islands, Rio de Janeiro (Brazil), Los Angeles (United States), Sydney (Australia), Dubai (United Arab Emirates), Tunis (Tunisia) and London (U.K.).

DAREDEVIL DIVER ■ At a Florida County Fair in 2008, Joe Egan of San Antonio, Texas, dove repeatedly from an 80-ft (24-m) platform into a pool 18 ft (5.4 m) deep—hitting the water at a speed of 60 mph (96.5 km/h). Filled with twists and flips, the dive took about two seconds and required him to enter the water feet first to avoid serious injury. Because of the impact, he could make the dive only 15 times a day.

SPRIGHTLY SPRINTER ■ In February 2008, Phillip Rabinowitz from Cape Town, South Africa, ran the 100 meters in 30.86 seconds—at the incredible age of 104.

ELDERLY GRADUATE ■ A 95-year-old great-grandmother graduated from college in 2007. Nola Ochs, who has 13 grandchildren and 15 great-grandchildren, received her bachelor's degree in General Studies and History at Fort Hays State University, Kansas.

BUNGEE JUMPS ■ New Zealander Mike Heard completed 103 bungee jumps from a bridge in just 24 hours in August 2008. He made his first 131-ft (40-m) plunge from Auckland Harbour Bridge head first, but soon changed to making the jump feet first to avoid getting unnecessarily wet.

YOUNG PROFESSOR ■ In 2008, New Yorker Alia Sabur was appointed a professor of physics at Konkuk University in South Korea—at the age of just 18. A child genius, she had earned her bachelor's degree at 14.

HIGH WIRE ■ Starting from opposite ends, Chinese high-wire walkers Adili and Ya Gebu passed each other on a single wire suspended more than 850 ft (259 m) above ground. Without safety wires or nets, they had to climb over each other in the middle of the wire that stretched almost three-quarters of a mile (1.1 km) over a valley in Gansu Province.

Eye-popping Ride

In 1954, Col. John Stapp of the U.S. Air Force found out what it feels like to travel from 0 to more than 600 mph (0–965 km/h) and back again in just a few seconds. Experimenting with the effects of G-force on the human body, he was strapped into a rocket-propelled sled on rails for the ride of his life. When the rockets were lit, the sled sent him from a standstill to 632 mph (1,017 km/h)—faster than a speeding bullet—in five seconds flat. It then hurtled into a water barrier and decelerated to a dead stop 1.4 seconds later. The force of this impact on Stapp's body felt like hitting a brick wall. His eyeballs shot forward in their sockets giving him two black eyes and temporary blindness. Pressure equivalent to 40 times the pull of gravity was exerted on his 168-lb (76-kg) body, making it weigh, for a moment, the equivalent of a staggering 6,720 lb (3,050 kg).

David Blaine had an amazing view of the sights over New York's Central Park—hanging upside down 40 ft (12 m) in the air for 60 hours, like a human bat. Doctors feared that he risked medical problems after such a prolonged spell the wrong way up, including losing his sight, but at the end of his stunt, Blaine dived from a 44-ft-high (13.4-m) platform, touched the ground for a moment and was then carried into the night sky by giant balloons.

HANGING TOUGH

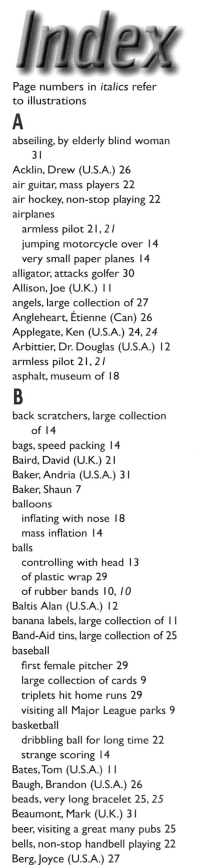

Index

Page numbers in *italics* refer to illustrations

ACKNOWLEDGMENTS

COVER (l) Rob Thomson; BACK COVER William T Knose Jr; 4 Rob Thomson; 6 (l)) Lucas J. Gilman/Barcroft Media, (r) Darin Quoid; 6–7 (dp) Lucas J. Gilman/Barcroft Media; 7 (r)) Lucas J. Gilman/Barcroft Media; 8 Henryk T. Kaiser/Rex Features; 9 Mieke Zuiderweg/Landov/Pa Photos; 10 Joe Raedle/Getty Images; 11 LEGO and The LEGO logo are trademarks of The LEGO Group, here used with special permission. © 2009 The LEGO Group. © 2009 Lucasfilm Ltd & TM. All rights reserved; 12 (b/l) Barcroft Media, (c, b/r) Susan Fessler; 12–13 (sp) © Connie Wade/Fotolia.com; 13 (t) Kent Horner/NBAE via Getty Images; 14 Charles Sykes/Rex Features; 15 (t) Long Hongtao/AP/PA Photos, (b) Reuters/Claro Cortes; 16 Library of Congress; 17 (t) Time & Life Pictures/Mansell/Getty Images, (b) Library of Congress; 19 Keith MacBeth; 20 William T Knose Jr; 21 (t) Rob Thomson, (b) Linda Abrams, Ercoupe "Sky Sprite"; 23 ChinaFotoPress/Photocome/PA Photos; 25 Caters News Agency Ltd/Rex Features; 26–27 ©Jeffery R. Werner/IncredibleFeatures.com; 28 Elmer Martinez/AFP/Getty Images; 29 (b) Feature China/Barcroft Media; 30 Barry Bland/Barcroft Media; 31 Emmanuel Aguirre/Getty Images; 32 Keystone/Getty Images; 33 (sp) KPA/Zuma/Rex Features, (b) Bryan Bedder/Getty Images

Key: t = top, b = bottom, c = center, l = left, r = right, sp = single page, dp = double page

All other photos are from Ripley Entertainment Inc.
Every attempt has been made to acknowledge correctly and contact copyright holders and we apologize in advance
for any unintentional errors or omissions, which will be corrected in future editions.